Trance Above the Streets (poems)
The Tradition of the New

ARSHILE GORKY

Mayor LaGuardia, being handed the magazine *Art Front* which was published by the Left Wing Artists Union, with Gorky looking on. Sketch of Newark Airport Mural in background. c. 1937.

ARSHILE GORKY

THE MAN, THE TIME, THE IDEA

HAROLD ROSENBERG

GROVE PRESS, INC.   NEW YORK

To Elaine and Willem de Kooning

CONTENTS

1. The Artist as Intellectual   13
2. Identity and Make-Up   29
3. Under the Banner of History   53
4. The Notebook of Vision   97

Notes   119
Chronology of Gorky's life   120
"Fetish of Antique Stifles Art Here"   123
Stuart Davis, by Gorky   127
The WPA Murals, statement by Gorky   130
Camouflage, course note by Gorky   133
"Farewell to Arshile Gorky,"
  poem by André Breton   136
Selected Bibliography   138

LIST OF ILLUSTRATIONS

Mayor LaGuardia, Gorky and Newark
  Airport Mural   *frontispiece*
Landscape   *page* 15
The Liver Is the Cock's Comb (colorplate)   18
The Artist and His Mother   21
Gorky in 1927   23
Drawing (Head, Dog and Anatomical Part)   25
Portrait of Ahko   27
Drawing   31
Objects   33
Pitcher and Fruit   35
Agony (colorplate)   38
Nighttime, Enigma and Nostalgia   41
Gorky and Willem de Kooning   43
Organization   45

Personage   47
Birth of the Nation   49
Xhorkom   51
Image in Xhorkom   55
The Limit (colorplate)   58
Enigmatic Combat   61
Painting   63
Gorky in 1938   65
Painting   67
Garden in Sochi   69
Garden in Sochi   71
Portrait of Mougouch   73
Anatomical Blackboard   75
The Plow and the Song (colorplate)   78
Painting   81
They Will Take My Island   83

Waterfall   85
Untitled Color Sketch   87
Water of the Flowery Mill   89
Virginia Landscape   91
The Unattainable   93
Diary of a Seducer   99
Frederick Kiesler, Gorky, Maria Martins,
    Marcel Duchamp, and Madame Donati   101
The Calendars   103
Gorky with Marc Gorky and André Breton   105
Drawing for The Betrothal   107
Study for The Betrothal   109
The Betrothal II   111
Soft Night   113
Making the Calendar   115
Composition   117

1

THE ARTIST AS INTELLECTUAL

BY WHATEVER MEASURE one ranks the founders of contemporary American abstract art, Arshile Gorky has a place on the top row. In different ways, he influenced several who were to become most influential: de Kooning, Pollock, Rothko, Nakian. His own work is almost a visual metaphor of the digestion of European painting on this side of the Atlantic and its conversion into a new substance. Not least, Gorky supplied a definitive image in the *romance* of post-War American painting: his embattled apprenticeship in Greenwich Village and Union Square, his sudden rise to fashionable Connecticut and the international art set, his sad end in a suicide motivated by illness, jealousy, and despair, constitute virtually the exemplary fable of the artist in our time. The familiar photograph of him, shot artistically from below, with great pensive black eyes, drooping mustache and leathery skin, situates him as a monument of melancholy in the hall of "modern American masters."

But though Gorky is a typical hero of Abstract Expressionism, his personality as well as his work refute generally accepted myths concerning this mode of painting, particularly the myth of an art that is an eruption of mindless energy. Above all, Gorky stands for the importance of intellect in painting—even in that kind of painting that verges upon automatism and draws upon buried sources. This lifelong student and, as Meyer Schapiro has recalled him, "fervent scrutinizer" of paintings, old and new, was an intellectual to the roots; he lived in an aura of words and concepts, almost as much at home in the library as in the museum and gallery. In her biography of the artist,[1] to which we owe so many carefully checked details, Ethel Schwabacher tells how Gorky carried "some small book of the masters with him at all times" and that he memorized the forms in the reproductions as one might lines of poetry. For Gorky, learning, analysis, hypothesis, were phases of his work as an artist, as drawing and painting were his means for understanding life and for trying out assumptions about it and about himself. One might say that the idea of getting the idea kept him busy from morning till night.

Gorky's career may be conceived as a succession

of dialogues with artists living and dead. One notes in his work echoes of Uccello, Ingres, Cézanne and, most dominantly, Picasso and Miró. Add to

Landscape. 1926-27. Oil. 16x20.
Collection Mr. & Mrs. Hans Burkhardt.

this his succession of friendships with painters— the early closeness to Mischa Reznikoff, his years of walking around with Willem de Kooning, his later attachment to Matta, the discourses he delivered on benches in Washington Square and in the cafeterias where artists hung out in the pre-War days—his most active hours were divided between hard talking and the labors of the studio. Perhaps "divided" is the wrong word, for he liked to talk even while painting. Yet Gorky was no chatterer; he argued values, attitudes, possibilities. Topics that might have entered a discussion as gossip came out subjected to judgment. He demanded of his talk that it have continuity with his deepest thinking, centered on art—when a fellow he had met at a party dropped in at his studio a day later merely to pass some time, Gorky turned him away through a crack in the door, saying, "You must be out of your mind!"

It was the shift of his verbal consciousness into the formulas of psychological experiment and magic brought to these shores by the Surrealists at the beginning of World War II that released Gorky's hand for the radical creations of the final period.

Both the temperament of Gorky and his procedures emphasize the intellectual ingredient in present-day American abstract art. From the early still lifes and portraits to the semiautomatic constructs of his last years, his paintings and innumerable drawings are reflective and imaginative, revealing in their consistently *soft* quality the gentleness of meditation, even when their imagery takes on the ferocity of dream libido. Gorky's submissiveness to the activity of understanding points to a motive entirely removed from that of "Expressionism." For him, the drama of art consisted in his striving to derive his character from his painting and from his thoughts concerning the traditional image of the artist, rather than in giving vent on canvas to

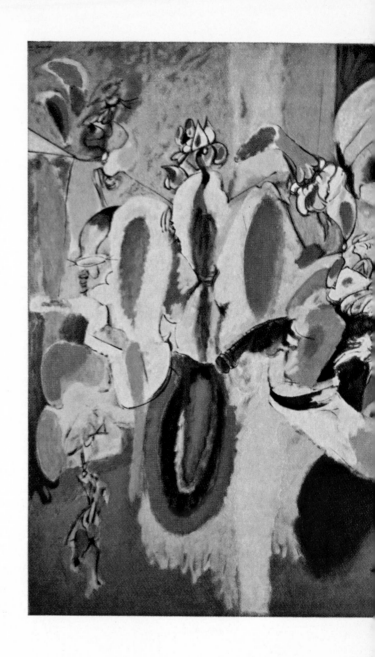

The Liver Is the Cock's Comb. 1944. Oil. 73 x 98.
Collection Albright-Knox Art Gallery, Buffalo.

motor impulses of personality. With Gorky, to be an artist counted far more than to be himself. Art was the promised land, in which he sought his

The Artist and His Mother. 1926-29. Oil. 60x50.
Collection Whitney Museum of American Art (gift of Julien Levy for Maro and Natasha Gorky in memory of their father).

place. He was a stranger to the temptation, common in this century, to blast off to an above and beyond of art—this was, probably, one of the deepest of his differences from the Surrealists. When, in his late drawings, he strewed the paper with fragments, letting both nature and composition take care of themselves, his wish was to bring forth not the random particles of an ego but evidences of the world evoked by his new esthetic consciousness.

No doubt art took on for Gorky so total a function because there was so little else in his life. An immigrant at an early age, he was one, moreover, who grew into manhood without strong folk or family environment. In his estrangement, however, he typified the condition that was to animate the new American painting, which is—though mention of the fact seems to embarrass some people— outstandingly *a newcomers' creation.* Immigrants and sons of immigrants predominate in the list of the originators of America's first identifiable style in art: de Kooning, Hofmann, Rothko, Gottlieb, Tworkow, Vicente, Baziotes, Lassaw, Guston, Reinhardt. Without the sharpened New World consciousness of the stranger, responding to the art crisis of the World War II decade, contemporary American art is inconceivable; and it is to that consciousness, in which uneasiness about the past is mixed with a radical sense of possibility, that it owes, in my opinion, its enthusiastic acceptance and emulation in nations undergoing drastic cultural change.

The immigrant is a self-made man. Making oneself (self-creation) is not, however, far distant from making oneself up (self-invention) and from make-up (self-disguise). When, on arriving in America, Gorky decided to become an artist, he decided at

Gorky in 1927,
New York City.

the same time to *look* like an artist. I place great importance on this comic-opera side of Gorky, sustained by his taste for an elegance tuned to the red plush era and by his Du Maurieresque appearance, tall, dark and handsome, with pleading war-orphan eyes. That this "Bohemian type," always ready to put on the neglected-genius act, especially in the presence of women and important people, should be at the same time a relentless thinker and disciplined creator is a puzzle designed to baffle moralizers and mislead swindlers.

Longtime apprentice-at-a-distance to Picasso, and later associate of the Surrealists driven to New York by the War, Gorky has been considered a "link" between 20th-century European art and present-day American abstraction. The notion is not without its usefulness. Gorky's work emphasizes the historical continuity of the new American painting, as against the illusion that it is a marvel (or monstrosity) sprung out of the American void (as if the void can give forth anything but history). In Gorky's paintings a provincial version of Paris Cubism visibly changes by combination with Surrealist-inspired data into something new.

The "link" idea slips, however, when it is applied to suggest that Gorky represents nothing more than a transition to a body of painting more "advanced" and more "authentically American" than his, a style born of native rawness and virility, perhaps one even cowboyishly Wild West. Those to whom Gorky represents a link to something newer and better should be reminded that in art, as elsewhere, a chain is nothing *but* links, and that there is no particular virtue in being the one at the end.

Gorky's art cannot be subsumed under anyone else's. Nor should it be forgotten that the "force" in some of our painting that has been taken to announce the presence of the American Eagle owes more to Vienna doctors than to the Rocky Mountains.

No more nor less in-between than any other contemporary, Gorky did, however, distinguish himself by taking hold of European art with max-

Drawing (Head, Dog and Anatomical Part). 1929. Pen. 22x29½. *Collection Mrs. Agnes Gorky Phillips.*

imum strength and in the widest range. "He was," de Kooning recently said about him, "a Geiger counter of art. In a room in the museum, he always ran to the right painting, and in the painting he always picked the really interesting thing." Gorky's self-training through voluntary servitude to a succession of masters was a subjective equivalent of the Renaissance mode of apprenticeship; everyone knows how fixed he was on Picasso throughout a decade. Less noticed is that during the same period he was equipping himself through study of other artists, including their personal oddities, to bring back alive into painting all sorts of insights, symbols, attitudes, which had been pushed aside in the common concerns of the day. At a time when the Cubist dogmas of "space," "flatness," and "tone" were clamped like an iron collar on American abstract art—as they still are on the brains of our critics—Gorky's researches were laying the ground for a broader way. One recalls the astonishment he aroused among Social Realists and Abstractionists alike when in a slide-lecture at the Artists Union in '36 or '37 he flashed on the screen, to illustrate a point about contemporary painting, the dragon wings and armor of a detail of an Uccello.

Painting today is a glamorous profession in America; as such it is bound to call attention to its heroes rather than to its ideas. For more than a decade, its ruling image has been that of the artist as a plunger of the unconsciousness who wins by a daring fling of the paint. No doubt, some of the new art was born with its eyes closed. Still, historical accuracy as well as the needs for the future demand that room be made for some countertypes.

Portrait of Ahko. c. 1930. Oil. 20½x15½.
Courtesy Sidney Janis Gallery, New York.

The model for one of these ought to be, without question, Arshile Gorky, whose ultimate pleasure was trying out theories and possibilities and who would not have abandoned his sobriety under the confetti of success.

2

IDENTITY AND MAKE-UP

GORKY'S LIFE seems organized for the convenience of the biographer. At the right time he was in the right place. In the Bohemian twenties he inhabited a studio on Sullivan Street in Greenwich Village. The year of the Wall Street Crash he moved to Union Square, where he remained throughout the decade of demonstrations, artists' unions, and government projects. The Depression at an end, he left the Square for Connecticut to become, amid the amenities of the International Set, an augur of the future prosperity of American art.

His natural inclination toward timeliness, by no means always productive of blessings, had put Gorky in touch with world history at an early age. Born in 1905 in Turkish Armenia of a family of village tradesmen and priests, his arrival on these shores was contrived by the war of 1914 and the subsequent cruelties of the Turks. The child of idyllic mountain pastures and lakes was torn from the closeness of Near Eastern clan life to be thrust across the globe as one of those "starving Armenians" whose misery made them the byword of an age of mass victims. By 1920, his mother dead, his family fallen apart, the fifteen-year-old refugee and a sister a year younger were attached to a party of immigrants and shipped off to America.

A succession of shocks and deracinations was the sum of Gorky's formative years. His ties with place and folk amputated, he passed in a single leap from feudal Asia to Western industrial megalopolis. It is this ordeal, abnormal but typical of the epoch, rather than some presumed childhood recollections of Byzantine church decoration, that, to my mind, laid the psychological ground for Gorky's spontaneous affinity with the vanguard schools of twentieth-century art, whose common feature is their jamming together of extreme time contrasts: the most primitive and the most advanced, voodoo and calculus, dream and obsessive systematization.

No doubt Gorky's fractured memories have a part in the moods of sadness and forlornness which he loved to elaborate in his social behavior. At the same time, the breach set his past at a distance, from which he could regard it with detachment. All his life Gorky took pleasure in trotting out as an exotic souvenir the Armenian peasant he might have been: he sang folk songs and did "shepherd" dances at drinking parties, wrote highly tinted, disconnected "recollections" of childhood, chose

Drawing. 1929-32. Ink. 14x17.
Courtesy Sidney Janis Gallery, New York.

his relatives as subjects of his early paintings, identified as his mother's butter churn a recurrent boot-like shape in his compositions. In playing the strayed Oriental, Gorky touched, of course, on authentic feelings; at the same time, he made a showman's use of a past that was to Americans a bag of oddities.

Stuart Davis in his irreplaceable memoir on Gorky[2] recalls that he and his artist friends turned thumbs down on the Armenian song and dance, and that "Gorky became aware of this ban very fast, and respected it after being properly indoctrinated in its rationale. He reserved his routine for other circles where it was appreciated and continued to go over big."

In any case, Gorky's background did not, as with Miró or Chagall, supply his paintings with a set of emblems, a glossary of exotic signs; nor, despite his social mannerisms, did there ever appear in his work any significant quantity of nostalgia or self-pity, beyond his endless nostalgia for masterpieces. The "local color" of his paintings, the environmental substance of their images, derives, from beginning to end, strictly from Gorky's esthetic experience. His Armenian childhood became, in sum, a decorative motif on the identity he chose for himself in deadly earnest; that of vanguard artist. Gorky lived *forward* into painting's last word; in the art of earlier centuries he looked for what lay ahead for contemporary painting—a way of reading history for events-to-come peculiar to artists, prophets, and gamblers. Gorky's "modernist" mental cast is already clearly defined in the tribute to Stuart Davis which he wrote in 1931, wherein he lauds intellectual, even mathematical, discipline, the modern age, modern art; admires Davis for the "definite and developed statement of his thoughts"; sees Picasso, Léger, Kandinsky,

Juan Gris as "bringing to us new utility, new aspects, as does the art of Uccello"; and goes on to challenge those who would brush these developments aside: "we shall not," says Gorky, "contrary to the expectations of these people, hear of the sudden death of cubism, abstraction, so-called modern art. These critics, these artists, these spectators who wait for a sudden fall are doomed to

Objects. 1932. Pen, brush and ink. 22¼x30.
Collection Museum of Modern Art.

disappointment." (With Gorky's English in mind, Davis doubts that Gorky could have written this piece himself, though Gorky always insisted that he had; yet Davis, too, is satisfied that Gorky's "way of thinking" is recognizable in it.)

Gorky's first five years in the United States continued an existence guided chiefly by external happenings: a short stay with his estranged father in Providence, a job in a rubber factory in Watertown, work as a sketch artist in a Boston theatre, attending classes in a technical high school. In the disorder of shifting for himself, the decision was formed to become an artist. Finding in Providence a pal in Mischa Reznikoff, a fellow-immigrant who was an art student, helped the decision along. Reznikoff, a little man, especially in contrast with Gorky's six feet two or three, and running over with gossip and "angles," as against Gorky's gnawing at themes, was the first in a series of psychic "partnerships" entered into by Gorky with other artists, all strangers in this country—as will be evident, I have yielded to the temptation to see in the small, volatile, resourceful Matta, who played so large a role in Gorky's last years, a "repetition" of Reznikoff.

Once reached, the resolution to make himself a painter took full possession of Gorky; from the first moment, he was never to be less than fully engaged in it. Such a total choice was not as common among American artists of the twenties as it is in these days when art has become an officially recognized profession in the U.S. Painters tended to practice art part time, with a job or, later, a "cause" occupying much of their attention. With Gorky, though

he loved success and having his say in artists' enter-
prises, nothing could rival the easel, even tempo-
rarily. Davis relates how Gorky and he lost touch
with each other in 1934 because, despite the Depression, Gorky "still wanted to play." By "play"
Davis means that for Gorky, Depression or no Depression, artists' unions or no artists' unions, the
primary issue was still the way one applied paint

Pitcher and Fruit. c. 1932. Oil. 14x17.
Collection Mr. & Mrs. Hans Burkhardt.

on the canvas. In this attitude Gorky anticipated the attitude of the post-agitational era that gave birth to present-day American abstract art.

Gorky's devotion to painting probably went too deep; he was, one may suspect, taking shelter in art from the strange continent upon which he had been cast. I have this impulse of Gorky's in mind when, describing the paintings of his last period, I speak of their "sheltered space." "This place seems so big and unhappy because you are not here," he complained in a love letter fifteen years after his arrival in the United States. Five years later he repeated the same phrase to another girl: "This place seems so big." Deprived of a world of familiar things, Gorky made art his universe, as does an immigrant the narrow routine of his shop. He stocked his studio with art supplies, as if he intended to hole up there for a siege—artists in the Depression marvelled at his huge inventory of paints, brushes, drawing papers, bolts of canvas.

In choosing his vocation, the immigrant chooses whom he shall become. It is not uncommon for him to celebrate this act by renaming himself. The Armenian refugee, Vosdanig Adoian, became an American artist under the name of "Arshile Gorky." The choice is an interesting one and demands analysis, especially since the question of identity is outstanding in regard to Gorky's paintings.

The important element is the surname borrowed from the celebrated Russian novelist. A bit of hesi-

*Agony. 1947. Oil. 40 x 50½. Collection The Museum
of Modern Art, New York (A. Conger Goodyear Fund).*

tation is to be noted in the "Arshile": at first, it
turns up as "Arschile," "Arshele," and "Arshille"

Nighttime, Enigma and Nostalgia. 1934. Oil. 36x48.
Collection Martha Jackson Gallery.

(one wonders why not "Achilles")—even after he
had settled its spelling Gorky never used it in sign-
ing his canvases; he deemed sufficient a neat, tiny
"A. Gorky," when he signed them at all. According
to friends, the artist had considered some "typical
American names," one being "Archie Gunn" in

tribute to the Western hard guy. But the name of an artist won out, moreover that of an artist of great reputation. (See article on Stuart Davis, Appendix.)

Becoming "Gorky" publicly transformed the Armenian villager into a cultivated Russian, a type of self-promotion according to homeland (rather than American) concepts of status typical of immigrants. By this name Gorky both affirmed his break with his past and placed himself under a halo of an artistic distinction which he had still to earn. It was a form of fakery that would compel him to move forward by sticking his neck out. Shortly after coming to New York, the young stranger palmed himself off in a newpaper interview[3] as the cousin of the famous writer and delivered himself of high-toned opinions about American women, skyscrapers, and the future of art in this materialistic country; incidentally, he claimed to have studied painting in Paris, like any good Russian. (See biographical note to "Camouflage," Appendix.)

"Maxim Gorky" was also, of course, a pseudonym. In making someone else's alias his own name Arshile involved himself in that higher mathematics of pseudonymity which was to be characteristic of his art. All through his career, his own inventions were ·to take off under the protection of a Name: Picasso, Miró, Matta—suggesting that he was never truly confident of making it on his own. At every stage, his work contains elements that will only come fully into the fore several years later under the guise of being borrowed from a more eminent artist, as if he had not the courage to stake out a claim to them. Perhaps his non-European origin made him anxious—who ever heard of an Armenian Michelangelo or Watteau?

Gorky and Willem de Kooning. c. 1935.

Perhaps the general inferiority-feeling of artists in New York vis à vis the Parisian "real thing" was in him exaggerated by the largeness of his aims—that timid little "A. Gorky" was the signature of a man who could conceive himself only in relation to the greatest. . . . In any case, one cannot speak of Gorky without the question of originality coming up—it is as if he personified the problem of who's who in a work of art. This, of itself, sets him on a plane of the highest esthetic interest, except for ideologists of Expressionism for whom the ultimate is a fingerprint. Gorky copies Picasso, who parodies Ingres, who was engaged in hiding something. The artist's masquerade resembles that of art itself, in which a constructed image, to begin with a "copy of nature," keeps reappearing for centuries in a succession of metamorphoses. Gorky's act of labeling himself with another man's device lies at the root of his processes as a painter and the metaphorical art that blossomed out of them.

For "the raw youth" to have a famous name had also its possibilities for comedy. Visiting a gallery together, Gorky and de Kooning ran into Eilshemius, who undertook to introduce them to a dealer. "This," he said, indicating de Kooning, "is—"

"Willem de Kooning," that artist hastened to fill in as the old man hesitated.

"Of course," acknowledged Eilshemius. "And this," he announced triumphantly, "is Mr. Tolstoy."

At the age of twenty-one, artist Gorky firmly presented himself in Greenwich Village, and soon became an instructor at the Grand Central Art School uptown. Former students remember him as a popular teacher, who stressed getting emotion

Organization. 1933-36. Oil. 49¾x60.
Courtesy Sidney Janis Gallery, New York.

into a drawing and underlined the point by bringing a Hungarian violinst to fiddle for the class. In the five years of his instructorship, Gorky tried out a variety of roles in the social comedy of the Young Master: for a while he wore a coat with a fur collar and passed as a successful European portrait painter. At other times, he raised a huge beard and played the lone Bohemian.

Davis, who met Gorky in 1929, describes him as possessing "a tall, dark and impressive aspect easily identifiable with the 'artist-type'. . . . He brought this asset to its maximum intensity by the adoption of a black velour hat pulled low over the eyes, and a black overcoat buttoned tight under the chin and extending to the ankles. The effect of this powerful disguise was excellently demonstrated by the terror it inspired in children when first confronted with it." Davis goes into detail about Gorky's "jive" English, "no mere matter of a simple foreign accent, although that was present, but an earthquake-like effect on sentence structure. . . . He was completely conscious of this bizarre linguistic collation, and on occasion messed it up still more in company where he thought it would be effective strategy." He inhabited, Davis' memoir adds, "a fairly decent artistic-type studio."

American art at the close of the twenties also wore a costume and spoke in a foreign accent. U. S. painting was Parisian, and the Bohemian get-up, together with the Greenwich village simulation of the Left Bank of the Seine, carried a pledge of allegiance to whatever authority swayed the Boulevard Montparnasse.

Under these circumstances, Gorky's choice of Cézanne as his first master was by no means re-

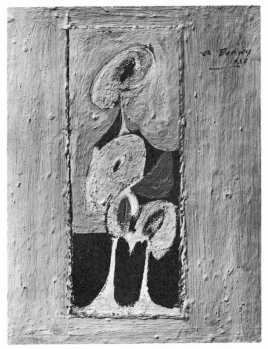

Personage. 1936. Oil. 8x10.
Collection J. J. Hirshhorn.

markable, any more than was his adherence to Picasso a few years later. Even for those to whom Cubism was nothing more than a café topic, Cézanne and Picasso loomed as the twin peaks of the School of Paris. A vanguard *will* sufficed to take a painter to one or both, as it did a writer to

Joyce or Proust. All that can be said of Gorky's early affiliation with Cézanne is that it was an instance of his speed in flying to the heart of the matter.

Nor was his way with the celebrated apples and brushed rocks the mark of a unique gift. Granted that he managed to lift the master's "look" by means of his own, this was to miss the aim inherent in those means. Yet Gorky's still lifes and landscapes of his Cézanne phase were unusual in two respects; in their extremely careful craftsmanship and in being *finished;* whereas the rule of young artists with advanced ideas was to play around ("experiment"), argue, give up and start elsewhere. Exhibiting a high, natural talent from the beginning, Gorky called attention to himself even more by his workmanlike approach.

It is in the early paintings of himself and members of his family, rather than in the still-life studies, that more obviously original features crop up, as if under the bidding of the past and the future. The animated shaping of the female head in *Portrait of Myself and My Imaginary Wife*, like the head, neck and hands of *Portrait of Ahko,* and the apron of the mother in *The Artist and His Mother,* worked on for years from a photograph, escape Gorky's current imitative intentions and foreshadow forms to emerge later (compare the shape of Ahko's face with the form of the lower right-hand corner of *Garden in Sochi* on page 69). Until his last years, no new idea ever shows itself in Gorky all of a piece; it pokes out, then recedes into the canon he is following. There is no end to his apprenticeship; yet at every stage, he reaches ahead to things of his own. Gorky's difficulty was never lack of invention; his lack went deeper:

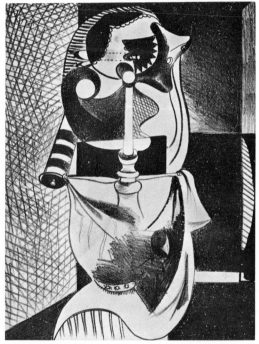

Birth of the Nation. 1936. Lithograph. 16x12. *Collection Mr. & Mrs. Hans Burkhardt.*

assertive as he was, he shrank from self-assertion and was timid in the face of what was uniquely his—a reticence not uncommon among creative egotists. His paintings of the twenties already give the hint in Gorky's art of a subterranean line of his own that will elude absorption by the styles he acquires.

In 1927 Gorky took the logical step from Cézanne to Cubism indicated by the history of twentieth-century art. Exhibitions of the Cubists had been increasing in New York; Gorky, a faithful gallery-goer and leafer through art magazines, soon put himself down as of the company of Braque, Picasso and Juan Gris. His still lifes of the next years show an ever-enlarging appropriation of the Cubist bag of tricks. At first, he simply arranges and rearranges shapes, as if they were cut-outs, building up each with layer upon layer of paint in a search for responsive variations of tone and the suggestion of mass through heavy texture. To these elements he later adds calligraphy superimposed on the forms but running across their contours. As his line establishes its rhythms with increasing independence he learns to use it to link shapes in space, producing constructions that play the eye back and forth between flatness and depth. Within a brief time, he has tried out the ambiguities of pasted-on paper and even, while still a Cubist, the sweet little butterfly wings of orthodox Surrealism.

Being the follower of a school could not, however, satisfy Gorky. He needed an individual master, since with him imitation was a learning to be, as well as a learning to do. Here, as with his name, Gorky's choice was loaded with significations. There are obvious reasons of reputation why Gorky should have picked Picasso to succeed Cézanne as his guide. Yet, in discipline and sense of rational purpose, his temperament had more in common with Braque's, to whom his work was already in debt. What held him apart from Braque

Xhorkom 1936. Oil. 36x48.
Courtesy Sidney Janis Gallery, New York.

was, it seems to me, the latter's sentiment of place. The Frenchman's lyrical celebration of familiar objects kept Gorky at arm's length; his own compositions concentrate entirely on "painting-elements"; when he sets up a bowl of flowers or a model, he denudes it of detail and environmental atmosphere, as in *The Artist and His Mother*. A distinction of Gorky's American Cubism is that it never applies itself to local themes like Max Weber's restaurants or Stuart Davis' road signs. It was the *abstractness of Gorky's personality*, in its context of estrangement, that attracted him more deeply to the Spanish sojourner in Paris than to the French modernist continuator of French taste. The thirties were to test the international idea. By 1930 Gorky had made himself the apprentice of the most international of painters.

3

UNDER THE BANNER OF HISTORY

The Idea of a Master

FOR GORKY, imitating Picasso meant not only a way of painting but of approaching world culture. This master taught by example that the artist today ought to be a living embodiment of the entire history of art. In our time each new work must constitute a decision as to what is living and what is dead in the painting of the past. The artist's rumination upon the history of art is thus a rumination upon himself as well, upon his taste, his intellectual interests, social judgments, the symbols that move him. Not individual genius but this double rumination of the artist upon his esthetic legacy and upon his own appropriation of it is the source of meaningful creation in this epoch of historical self-consciousness. A style truly modern must be capable of mirroring the paintings and carvings of all times and places: ancient Greece, Renaissance Europe, the African jungle. Recognizing that art has become the collective property of mankind and that all belongs to each, the artist seeks this inspiration in the common store. He is, first of all, a critic, whose meditations on the canvas give rise to an art of a new dimension: that of art's own awareness of what it has been and is. . . . It is generally acknowledged that Gorky was a great connoisseur of painting; what is overlooked is that becoming one was part of his Picasso discipleship.

The vision of the work of art as a reanimation of existing art was perhaps the most profound and productive esthetic idea of the first two decades of this century. It was an idea with deep roots in literature as well as painting; it reached back to Rimbaud's discovery of the esthetic virtues in "poetic old junk" and to Mallarmé's systematic investigation of the lyrical accretions of certain words; it was present in Cézanne's reclaiming of Poussin in nature. Among literary contemporaries of Picasso, it widened into Joyce's rewriting of Homer and of the tongues of man as immediate experience in Dublin, into Pound's slang-spangled translations of the poetry and manners of ancient cultures, into Eliot's indissoluble formula of the poem as an "objective correlative" wherein the poet's emotion takes on a new life by entering the tradition of poetry.

In both painting and literature, art as resurrection of art gave prominence to three formal prin-

Image in Xhorkom. c. 1936. Oil. 32⅞x43.
Collection Miss Jeanne Reynal.

ciples: allusion, parody, quotation. Of these, the first is the most profound, the true ghostly principle of historical revival, since by allusion the thing alluded to is both there and not there; while parody or quotation brings the original work forward either in a distorted form or as a passage in a different work.

Allusion is the basis upon which painting could, step by step, dispense with depiction, without loss of meaning: on the contrary, depiction, as was already well realized in the nineteenth century, could be an obstacle to communication of the artist's meaning, besides having had its age-old mystery extracted by the camera. To the degree that depiction gave way to various systems of allusion—emotional reference evoked by color, by shape, by movement—"abstract" art became possible. In this century, every major work of art, whether pictorial or not, is charged—the word is Ezra Pound's—with allusion: to things or events, read, dreamed or half-remembered, but, above all, to high points in the history of its medium.

Parody and quotation are forms of allusion that remain chained to specific work, rather than awakening associations in the whole symbolic field. Mimicking existing works and taking extracts from them have always, of course, been practices in art. To the history-conscious artist of this century, however, both parody and quotation assumed new depth; he resorted to the take-off and to insertions of lifted passages for his most serious effects, as in Picasso's Grünewald *Crucifixion* or Miró's *Dutch Interior* series. These reflections of other works had nothing in common with plagiarism, since the loot-

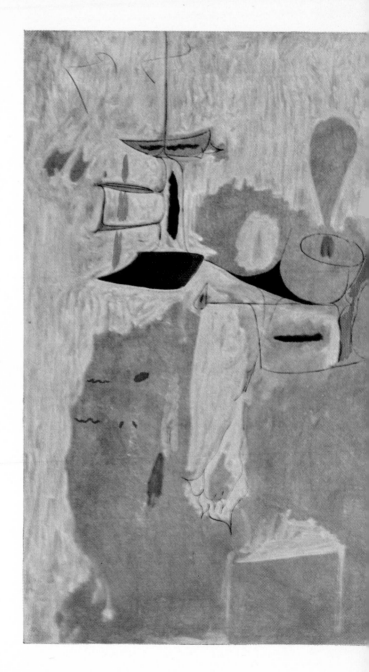

The Limit. 1947. Oil. 50½ x 62¾. *Courtesy Sidney Janis Gallery, New York.*

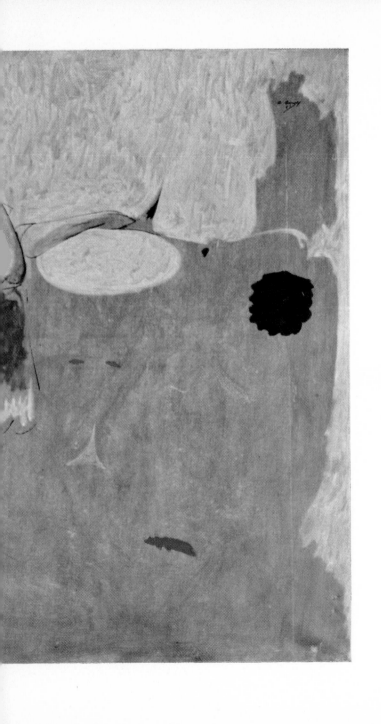

ing was intended to be spotted and the original object thus brought into the new context, as in a

Enigmatic Combat. c. 1936. Oil. 35¾x48.
Collection San Francisco Museum of Art (gift of Miss Jeanne Reynal).

Cubist collage, the most extreme example of quotation in painting.

Allusion, parody, and quotation cut across all contemporary schools (with the possible exception of Neo-Plasticism, though Mondrian regarded his compositions as distinctly allusory); they are as prevalent in Fauvism as in Dadaism or Expressionism, in Léger as in Bertolt Brecht: they introduce into the diversity of this century's modes the unity of the style called "modern." They are forms through which is asserted the uneasy intuition of this epoch that "real" art belongs to other times and places, to communions destroyed by our revolutionary age: but through which is asserted at the same time the counter-intuition that art is deathless and that it actually rises to new heights in becoming nothing else than the artist's experience of it. Allusion expresses both the despondency of modern art and its enthusiasm, its awareness of itself as "counterfeit" as well as its clarified assurance of the inferior significance of all less history-conscious productions.

All through the thirties Gorky was a parodist and "quoter"—first of Picasso, then of Miró, with side glances at Masson and Léger. It was to take a full decade for his art to pass from mimicry of other artists to the poetry of allusion, and from the "rhetoric" of the individual master to an independent utilization of the common alphabet. While it is true that Gorky's Picasso imitations bore his unique imprint, particularly in his use of color, this did not give them a voice of their own: hang a Gorky of this period next to a Picasso, the latter does all the talking while the Gorky patiently lip-reads.

Those eager to claim early originality for Gorky contradict Gorky's values. At twenty-five he had grasped the basic premise of the art of this time, and had grasped it with the energy and curiosity of one who has no heritage he can take for granted and to whom all knowledge is consequently brand new. This premise he restated in its most dramatic form: *the deliberate rejection of originality.* How

Painting. 1936-37. Oil. 38x48.
Collection Whitney Museum of American Art.

highly original a thing this was to do, Stuart Davis testifies in a passage notable for its hard accuracy and strength of feeling:

> During the period that I knew him, Gorky's work was strongly influenced by certain styles of Picasso. This was apparent to everybody, and there was a tendency to criticize him as a naive

imitator. I took a different view and defended his work at all times. Admitting the influence, I would challenge the artist-critic on his own imitation of corny ideas about the old masters, Cézanne or some appeasement splinter-group of modernism, instead of the real thing.

Davis himself seems rather to have missed the "acculturating" process in Gorky's imitation, that is, his use of Picasso as a key to open for him the work of other artists, schools, and periods; he conceives it as a mere phase in the technical training of "a talented artist in the process of development." Gorky, however, was not simply trying to make himself into a good Cubist painter, as Davis, for one, had already succeeded in doing. Had his aim been merely to qualify as a member of the school, his identification with Picasso would have been far too complete. He does not, like other abstract artists of the day, seek his own Cubist note, nor does he Americanize Picasso by substituting banjos for guitars. On the contrary, Gorky paints precisely guitars, so that his being influenced is "apparent to everybody." He strives to make his own every gesture of the master, like the holy disciple described by Martin Buber who did not come to hear wisdom from his teacher but "to see how he unlaces his felt boots and laces them up again." With a tremendous intuition of true discipleship, which demands the abnegation of personality, Gorky saw that the point was to make the beginning of a tradition in himself. His paintings and innumerable drawings of that period are not so much imitations of Picasso's canvases as impersonations of Picasso's

Gorky in 1938, New York City.

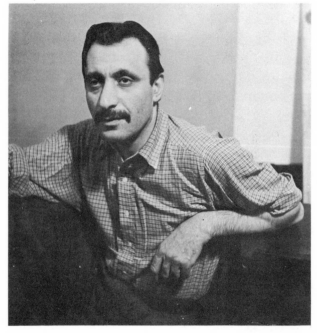

(Photo: Wilfrid Zogbaum)

behavior before the easel or drawing board. The aim was to be able to mistake himself for Picasso, so as to be able, spontaneously, to "do a Picasso" that would be a new work. For to him Picasso was not simply a great artist but the personification of art balancing itself on the present moment.

Through this master lay the way to the next historical step beyond him.

Here Gorky's play-acting shows its serious side by giving reality to the part chosen by his imagination. He stands up publicly to the ridicule of being the Picasso of Washington Square, as he had stood up to the farce of being an important Russian. When, in '37, some important paintings arrived in New York in which the Spaniard had allowed the paint to drip, artists at the exhibition found a chance for their usual game of kidding Gorky. "Just when you've gotten Picasso's clean edge," one said in mock sympathy, "he starts to run over."

"If he drips, I drip," replied Gorky proudly, though by that time he was no longer clinging to Picasso's details.

Willem de Kooning, who met Gorky around 1934, emphasizes the impact upon him of Gorky's discounting the idea of originality. After a few encounters in the street, he brought Gorky to his studio and showed him some drawings. Examining them, his new friend put them down and remarked, "Aha, so you have ideas of your own."

"Somehow," de Kooning recalls, "that didn't seem so good."

In de Kooning's recollection, Gorky's raising this question changed his entire attitude toward painting. If you had your own idea, that was it, you were stuck with it. The history of painting, however, contained endless inventions which the living painter could make his own. Even inventing a thing that had already been invented was an act of creation. De Kooning likes to call this "inventing the harpsichord"—the fact that we have the harpsi-

Painting. 1938. Oil. 29x40.
Courtesy Sidney Janis Gallery, New York.

chord, and even the piano that superseded it, does not prevent the invention that brought it into being from being legitimately repeated. This, apparently, was Gorky's principle. De Kooning says he went home after his new friend's reaction to his originality and thought over his own position. Have not his paintings since been supreme examples of the double reference: to direct personal experience and to current developments in painting conceived in relation to their historical direction?

The two artists carried on their dialogue for years, in their studios, on the street, at lunch counters. They worried every possibility like a pair of hungry dogs. Each brought important powers to the collaboration. One inclines to accept Thomas Hess's judgment that Gorky excelled in awareness of what was happening in art, de Kooning in regard to the artist's means. As a theoretician Gorky was inexhaustible; nothing could stop the flow of his speculation—the evening he told me about the terrible cancer that was soon to contribute to his death he went on to develop a notion, for which he claimed support in "early English writers," to the effect that boredom was the truest source of artistic inspiration. On the other hand, there was not a trick of the painter's trade that de Kooning did not have up his sleeve; often it was from this sleeve that the "trade" acquired it. One day, after Gorky had become attracted to Miró, de Kooning found him cursing his inability to paint a long thin line. He was trying to do it with his "fat Rubens brushes," and de Kooning was amazed to learn that Gorky had never heard of the sign-painters' liner brush. Having bought one, de Kooning remembers, Gorky sat around all day in an ecstasy painting long beautiful lines.

De Kooning has paid the warmest tribute to Gorky's uncommon sense of vocation. Living in the Depression upon bits gathered from private pupils, dinner invitations, small loans, Gorky managed to keep foremost the artist-image even in his physical surroundings. When he entered Gorky's studio in the not-very-clean building at 36 Union Square, de Kooning has written, "the atmosphere was so beautiful that I got a little dizzy and when

Garden in Sochi. 1938-41. Oil. 25x29.
Courtesy Sidney Janis Gallery, New York.

I came to, I was bright enough to take the hint immediately."[4] With the photos of Uccellos and Ingres tacked on the wall, everything (including the art-store quantities of paint and canvas mentioned above) stacked in place, the brushes cleaned after each use, floor scrubbed each week end, the studio was a hideout of art beyond time, place and circumstance. De Kooning wonders whether Gorky's neatness had something to do with his being an Armenian; on the other hand, it was de Kooning's own countrymen who gave their name to a cleanser. Be that as it may, de Kooning's description of his friend's quarters is of the first importance in estimating the saving role of art in Gorky's life. The affectionate care he devoted to his surroundings in the thirties is hardly consistent with the bleak despair and soul-crushing isolation he is said to have suffered in those years. One can only guess that some of his later intimates have taken at too close to face value Gorky's pose of *artiste assassiné* with its ordeal by starvation and neglect.

From Picasso Gorky learned: above all, keep at it. If you have no ideas, draw the model. If you have no model, copy reproductions. If you are depressed, draw; if you get drunk, go home and start a picture. If there is shooting outside the window, go on drawing. For the artist, there is only one real situation, and only one salvation: art.

In Gorky's work of this period meticulousness

reaches the point of obsession. He carries to completion composition after composition on the same themes, always in search of the perfect approximation to the work of the master. His drawings in ink run, in the space of a year, into the hundreds, into the thousands. Darkened areas are often

Garden in Sochi. 1941. Oil. 44¼x62¼.
Collection Museum of Modern Art.

knitted of myriad cross-hatchings, carefully toned; the manual routine no doubt had a soothing influence, detaching him from the concentrated anxiety of his intellectual quest. Works are finished to the last detail on expensive imported paper, yet once done they represent for him mere exercises. Several witnesses support the story told in Elaine de Kooning's pioneer article on Gorky[5] of the artist niggling for weeks at an ink sketch for a WPA mural, stroke by measured stroke; finished at last, he straightens his aching back, grabs a sponge, soaks it full of water and, as is his custom, swishes it back and forth over the drawing to smooth down the surface. In this drawing, alas, the ink dissolves and the forms run together— ruined. He had gotten his ink bottles mixed on the drawing table. Gorky looks into the dismayed eyes of his friends and after a minute announces: "I didn't like it anyway."

There is one aspect of Picasso that Gorky never emulated: I refer to the master's lampooning of art itself. Self-conscious as he was about becoming an artist, levity about painting was beyond Gorky, to say nothing of flashes of rage or disgust at the whole enterprise of creation. He was never art's bad boy; his parodies were never lightened by the comic spiirt. Deliberate bad drawing, purposeful vulgarity, self-caricature—for these Gorky lacked the sense of security and aristocratic scorn.

Periodically, he dropped piles of his drawings into the ash can and put his feet through scores of canvases. At one time he spread the word that any painting in his studio was for sale for $25. Many of the extant Gorkys of the period are rescued works, discards picked up by his students or lightly acquired for a few dollars by good-natured acquaintances.

Gorky's paintings of this phase were try-outs; on the one hand, tests of his ability to give his canvases the look of contemporary masterpieces, as he had, with some awkwardness, given himself

Portrait of Mougouch. 1941. Oil. 8x10.
Collection J. J. Hirshhorn.

the look of The Artist; on the other hand, experiments with the possibility that through an effort of will he could force the emergence of a clue to the necessary next step in painting. Like his early idol Uccello, Gorky was wrestling with the problem of art in his age: what would art be tomorrow? Uccello, too, had found his problem waiting for him; he hadn't invented spatial perspective any more than Gorky had invented the perspective of the crystal ball; he was merely its fanatic—as Mary McCarthy says in her book on Florence, "fascinated by perspective [he] was the first 'cracked' artist of modern times." Friends who urged Gorky to "get away from Picasso" must have thought at times that he was cracked too—and the parallel holds as far as the *uccello* (bird) that became one of his favored images.

The problem of the artist had become a total one: no longer to explore a "law of nature" but to qualify as the vehicle of the evolution of art. Time, one might say, had superseded order, terrestrial and divine alike, as the arbiter of esthetic values. A Dadaist who, *at the right moment*, had pasted some bus transfers between smears of blue was already assured of an immortality certain to be denied to the dutiful heir of traditional methods. To survive—and survival is the only proof accepted by history that one has existed—the artist had now to find the means to shove himself into the historical line-up. These means were neither technical nor intellectual; in fact, it was plain that no one knew, nor could know, what they were. With the practice of art thus turned into a gamble —celebrated by Mallarmé in *Un Coup de Dès*—

artists crowded around the table in search of history's winning combination.

Gorky's obsessive self-training was an attempt to minimize the risk imposed by history. Since

Anatomical Blackboard. 1943. Pencil and crayon.
19⅞x27½. *Collection Walter Bareiss.*

except for being an artist he was nothing, he stood to lose too much should the future rule that his work had turned up a blank. Perhaps by patiently beating his way up and down behind the backs of the sure winners, he might find a spot to slip in among them. Emulating Picasso, he kept an eye on the Surrealists, while floating repeatedly back to Cézanne in outdoor sketches done in Central Park. Prophetic insights, as well as accidental effects, were abandoned after a shot or two if no way appeared to assimilate them into the Parisian canon. His head full of notions, Gorky drew back from giving himself to any of them, as against the large note that art seemed to him about to sound in his time. His own ideas were treated as hardly serious conceits to be discharged in talk, as when he would demonstrate to listeners in Union Square how a line could follow the movement from a cloud down to the rooftops and into the street to the park bench where they sat.

In this cautious way Gorky was able by 1936 to move from Cubist construction, conceived in a spirit of intellectual certainty rare in the art of this country, to an idiom paced by sweeping organic forms. As befitted this artist who loved to teach and explain, the development was a logical one. The new paintings are a version of Cubism, and they could have been an individual one. It happened, however, that André Masson had gotten there first; to Gorky, this no doubt made the step legitimate. Once again, he not only produced a derivation but felt the need to signal the fact by taking over Masson's heart shape and by echoing in his titles the Frenchman's *Cock Fight* and *Battle of the Birds*.

To a notable degree, working in his new form freed Gorky from the studio as subject matter;

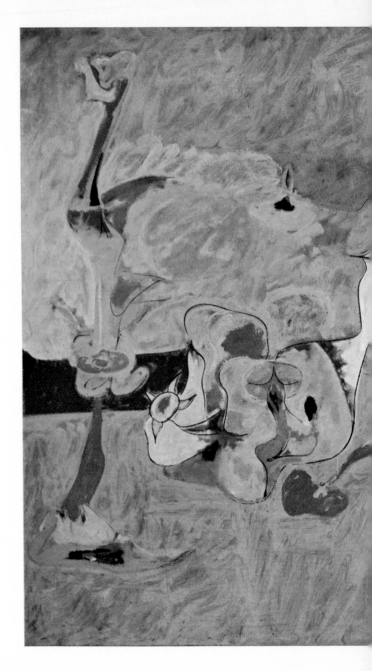

The Plow and the Song. 1947. Oil. 52 x 64.
Collection Mr. and Mrs. Milton A. Gordon.

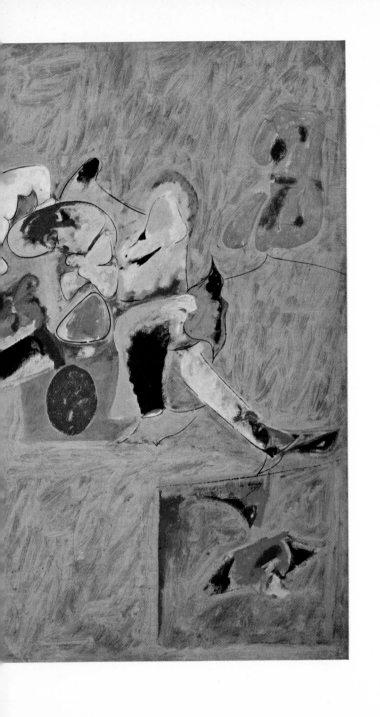

shapes that were before strictly elements of composition now appear as symbols. His imagery begins to reach back into the verbal world of poetry and into the erotic. The bird is adopted as a strong motif (the bird's eye had shown up in earlier pen and ink drawings), and the rhythm of the shapes affirms the idea of action—though the "enigma" of *Enigmatic Combat* may well consist in this picture's being an accounting with Picasso.

Painting. c. 1943. Oil. 20x25½.
Collection Miss Jeanne Reynal.

Gorky's agitated abstractions of 1936-38 have a denser emotionality than Masson's and a more rugged conviction in their drawing and application of paint; in fact, the thickness of his pigment now conflicts oddly with the intermixing of indefinite shapes which he permits himself for the first time. Both artists were on their way out of Cubism by the same route: the evocation of visual metaphors, e.g., animal organs growing out of plants. But while Masson's investigations of natural correspondences were soon to fall into systematization, to Gorky each sign would continue to hold the possibility of being a hint regarding himself.

Yet before such hints could be followed up, art history had to be pursued to the end. Having hesitatingly let go of the coattails of Picasso, Gorky found himself clutching those of Miró. Here again the tendency of friends is to "defend" Gorky by searching for differences: given his idea of going through the master to the point past him, these can have only a casual interest. Nothing could have been farther from Gorky's procedures than Miró's dashing automatism of those days. His iconography strengthened Gorky in his own adoption of sign language, but the latter's move toward memory carried no deeper than the use he found for it in his art. Gorky's "Mirós" are, like his Picassos, products of experimental research, not of dream expanded by autobiographical association. Each of the different versions of *Garden in Sochi* is a rap upon a different stylistic door *to the future,* and a disappointed turning away when no answer comes. We can see today that the 1942 *Garden* was a sufficient opening through which

They Will Take My Island. c. 1943. Oil. 38x48.
Collection Miss Jeanne Reynal.

unexplored regions might have been reached.
Unfortunately, history when it does supply answers
never labels them as such.

Left Bank Versus Left Front

The decade of the Depression and totalitarian-
ism that ended in World War II did not doubt
that art was inspired by history. But which history? The history of art, following its own logic,
for example that which led from Cézanne through
Cubism to Mondrian? Or the history of society,
which declared art to be a "reflection" of national

or class struggles, of popular myth, of an aristocratic or religious tradition?

To the close of the twenties, art had seemed to go its own way through a succession of "movements" opposing and complementing one another. Centered in Paris, an international of creation had been absorbing into its processes the esthetic productions of every stratum of world culture, from East Indian court painting to advertising and circus posters. Suddenly, the iron bands of economic and political crisis choked off this communion and with it the parturition of the schools. By 1929, Surrealism, the last of the Paris art movements, had stiffened and come apart. No successor appeared.

The Depression drastically transformed the American sector of the art international. With the drying up of their allowances, the expatriate painters and poets fled back to the paternal shores, where a new sobriety quickly put the Bohemias of New York, Chicago and the Coast on trial. Against the idea of an esthetic elite arose the concept of a political vanguard, with its morality of party and class allegiance. Soon the banner of the Left Bank cafés was transferred to the meeting halls of the Left Front, with corresponding adjustments in costume, insignia and ideology.

The new Left categorically identified all the experimental schools as symptoms of the collapse of the middle class, as the Right had for almost a century denounced vanguard art as a cultural conspiracy of the Left. Social radicalism now

Waterfall. c. 1943. Oil. 60½x44½.
Courtesy Sidney Janis Gallery, New York.

asserted the death of radical art and bade the artist exchange his investigative and experimental function for a firm role in a political movement of mass education and mass action.

Gorky and a minority of "playboys" held stubbornly to the principle that art had to pursue its own way, regardless of what Davis called "the mutual distress." Older Abstractionists, including Davis, for whom the way of art was already laid out, undertook the social role for a portion of themselves; they went on painting as before but signed up for "organizational work" in their spare time—one might have called them "Sunday revolutionists." Their splitting of art from action carried, of course, the suggestion that their work was either historically counterfeit or intellectually frivolous; and it was often denounced as such by the bosses of the Left (as was later that of Picasso during his membership in the Communist party), until the unprincipled *laissez faire* of the Popular Front provided official sanction for a vanguard marching under two flags.

For Gorky, as for de Kooning and a handful of others, the researches of art could not confine themselves to a niche set aside for them by an indifferent radicalism. If the Left had something to say about painting, what was it in terms of *painting?* If not, what good was a revolution that could not change your signature?

Gorky was not so much in opposition to the political environment as a man on its edge—with something a bit passé in his sad big-eyed glance, in his manners that were neither American nor "proletarian," in his secretiveness, his rich lady students. Clinging to his distant masters, his painting bore an embattled unrelatedness to events on the streets, the cries from the soap boxes, the

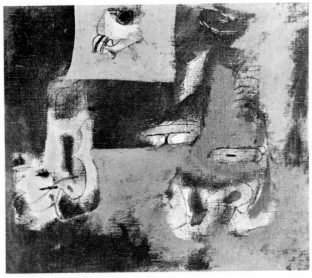

Untitled Color Sketch. 1944. Oil. 9¼x10⅝.
Collection Michael Blankfort.

enthusiasms of new dealers in socially "realistic" art. For a neighbor of the Co-op Cafeteria on Union Square, its walls covered with huge square-cut workers and gear shapes, to entitle a painting *Nighttime, Enigma and Nostalgia* was to make a public declaration of being out of step. Throughout the thirties Gorky's work constituted an actual testing of the degree to which art could enclose itself within its own realm.

This testing was the more extreme in that Gorky did not isolate himself from the New York art mass, including those who wished to make of painting a tool of social agitation. He had a continuing emotional interest in politics for its own sake, particularly in its drama. Moreover, he was ready to entertain the possibility that the Left might provide the clue to art's next move. Thus, on at least one occasion, Gorky took the lead in organizing a meeting of fellow artists to look for a "Marxist" approach to painting. For the chief negative contention of the social Front had to be granted: though Fauvists, Neo-Plasticists, Cubist, Expressionists, were to be met with at every turn, historically the advanced schools had closed their books. For the first time in a century, art had no place to go—except out into the world.

Thus Gorky and his friends nosed cautiously around the Left. Holding to the Left Bank notion of an independent history for art they were tempted by the Left Front vision of the artist as collaborator in the creation of living history. That the same inspiration would guide the hand with the brush that moved the hand on the lathe—the idea was well-nigh irresistible, especially in a time that felt so intensely the reality of food and shelter. If only this inspiration would show itself in a valid form of painting.

Water of the Flowery Mill. 1944. Oil. 42x48¼. Collection Metropolitan Museum of Art (George A. Hearn Fund, 1956).

Keeping the parties to the Left Bank-Left Front debate in close touch with each other was the art program of the Federal Government and the accompanying artists union that sprang up in connection with it. Gorky was in the first group of New York artists hired by the Civil Works Administration [later Works Progress Administration (WPA)] mural Project and he stayed on for several years. His Newark airport murals, done on the Project, illustrate the kind of values that during those years infiltrated the mind of even so "pure" an artist. The murals are an all-but-characteristic exhibition of Gorky's skill in playing variations on Cubist pattern-making. An anthology of "new design," they are an evasion of the then current Left mural art of Rivera and Orozco, on the one hand, and of the liberal patriotic reminiscence of Benton, on the other. As a commercial job in the latest modes of decoration (including photomontage), they were superb; as art, they were, by the standard of Gorky's easel painting during the same years, nil. What was pathetic was that even this display of neutralized skill had to be justified for its up-to-dateness before mayors and administrators and made an issue for protesting delegations, so that, without having fully considered what he was doing, the artist found himself pleading to be allowed to make himself socially useful.

The elaborate statement which Gorky prepared for WPA to explain the airport murals was the work of such a superimposed socially useful consciousness.[6] Almost every phrase could be preserved in a dictionary of esthetic clichés designed to flatter popular incomprehension. Taking Gorky at his word, we should have to conclude that airplanes rise into the ether so as to arrive at Léger.

Virginia Landscape. 1944. Ink and pastel. 14x19.
Courtesy Stephen Hahn Gallery, New York.

His "plastic problem" in regard to the murals, says Gorky, was how to introduce into the two dimensions of a wall "the unbounded space" of aviation, and this problem resolved itself "when I considered the new vision that flight had given to the eyes of man." What Gorky's argument amounted to was that he could paint flight on a wall because to one looking down from an airplane things look flat—which is "selling" Cubism with a vengeance as a new naturalism. In all, the statement is on a par with one Gorky prepared half a dozen years later for a course in camouflage, based on "the various branches of modern art [which] through exhaustive experiment and research have created a vast laboratory whose discoveries unveiled for all the secrets of form, line and color" (see Appendix). Both statements remind us that the play-actor and ideological prestidigitator in Gorky were brought out to protect him in the presence of society. They also exemplify the passion of American art twenty-five years ago to prove it had a place in man's progress, even in his increased capacity to kill himself.

Gorky's schizophrenia in regard to WPA was matched in other American artists to whom the art idea still came first. Almost to a man, they were allured by the social principle, at least to the point of allowing it to rule their public vocabulary. They were aware of the psychic corruption spread by modern utilitarian art-values, yet the realization was softened into dreamy acceptance by grandiose notions concerning the future role of painting in the rehabilitation of society.

Thus art in the thirties existed on the borderline of social action—for Gorky, wrapped up in his studies and his search for the new note, as for his contemporaries who lay down their drawing implements to enroll as volunteers in the Spanish Civil War. Can one doubt that it was the challenge to action on the streets that was to lead in the next decade to the response in practice that

The Unattainable. 1945. Oil. 41⅛x29¼.
Collection Barney Rosset.

the action of the artist took place on the canvas? To the pragmatic ideologies of the Depression the pragmatic response of art was to be Action Painting.[7]

Before a new move could be made, however, the Left Front in art had to finish itself off; by the end of the thirties this had been accomplished with remarkable thoroughness. The Stalin-Hitler Pact barred further assent to the fallacy that the "logic of history," particularly as formulated by a ruling political group, could animate the Muse of Painting; while the substitution of the U.S. Defense Program for "work relief" resulted in the recruiting of painters of dust bowls and city starvelings into government-agency poster squads. One thing had been resolved for our time: that, whatever the fate of the Left Bank, the Left Front was not the alternative.

Yet the esthetic idea still stood at an impasse. Crisis-torn Paris had been demonstrating for a decade the impotence of painting to spin a future out of itself in disregard of the conditions of its existence. The fall of the city to the Nazis closed off finally the source from which art could hope to continue to feed on art.

Neither post-Cubist abstraction nor Social Realism could meet the needs of painting in America. Undoubtedly, the paintings of Gorky were among the most esthetically perceptive of the time. Yet so long as his goal was to produce a picture that would stand alongside those of the European masters, his work could not transcend parody. The bankruptcy of a rationale of progress in regard both to art and to social history had to be acknowledged and an appeal addressed to other powers of the mind.

4

THE NOTEBOOK OF VISION

Gorky's timeliness again: in the year of Pearl Harbor everything changes for him. The flight of the Surrealists to this side of the Atlantic had begun and the Armenian immigrant welcomes the European exiles. The "abstract man" of the Village streets, nourishing himself on what his brain can extract from books and reproductions is drawn, step by step, into a living milieu the elements of which combine, like dream projections, his aspirations towards a place in the art of Paris and a position of professional dignity in the United States. In tune with an increasing animation in his paintings—in a 1941 version of *Garden in Sochi,* the forms ride loosely in looped contours and his characteristically loaded paint surfaces have given way to thin washes and illuminated tints—he meets a handsome girl, the daughter of a U.S. admiral, takes a trip to the West Coast, gets married in Nevada. Suddenly, the lonely Gorky has broken out of the Bohemian dogtrot, has a home, friends who buy his pictures and invite him to elegant houses; his summers are spent on the hundred-acre farm of his wife's parents in Virginia. In a preview of the future social elevation of American painting, the controversialist of the park bench and the cafeteria table has become, as American, a respected member of the international art world.

In the transformation of Gorky, the arrival in New York of the Paris artists was no doubt decisive. In their presence, art ceased to be an ideal, at bottom only half believable, and the artist a part to be played, half sham, half desperate hope. Art was *here*, and the artist a man like himself. The impact of the Surrealists, with their programmatic union of art and daily life, was especially invigorating in Gorky's new domestic situation.

Given this dramatic stimulus by the Europeans upon Gorky and a few other American painters, some critics have come to consider post-War U.S. art to be, as it was in the past, a mere local extension of School of Paris styles—had the Left Bank migrated to Brazil, a similar development would, presumably, have sprung up in São Paulo. The fact is, however, that, while there was much for the Americans to learn, there was nothing for them to "extend." The debarking of the fugitives upon

these shores coincided with an already-existing break in the continuity of European creation—the fall of Paris put the seal of force upon an epoch that was ended; when, after the War, the Parisians returned home they could only rearrange themselves in pre-War categories. In sum, having the Europeans in the neighborhood simply confirmed what the American artist already knew only too well from ten years of staring across the Atlantic: that the modern schools were played out and that a new move had to be made.

Yet by personal example the Parisians supplied the clue to what this move might be. Before the blank wall at which the art movements of the twentieth century had come to a stop, the Americans now saw a parade of single artists as the living residue of the Schools. Cubism, Fauvism, Futurism, Dada were dead, but Léger, Chagall, Ernst, Masson were working as vigorously as ever. The lesson to the Americans was for each to seek in himself for the the point of departure which they had sought with others in the history of art or in the history of society. Never mind finding the answer—the answer is the work itself.

What do Gorky's late paintings and drawings owe to Surrealism? To conceive him as "taking over" the style of the newcomers is to misconceive the relationship. As a manner of painting, Surrealism in 1940 was neither a force nor a novelty; in that heyday of Peter Blume, Surrealist pictures had become an expected ingredient in every all-

American annual. (See also Gorky's "Drawing," page 31.)

What the Surrealists could impart, and *only in person,* was their conception of the artist, one that happily contradicted the whole "objective" fixation of American painters. In a situation where all ideas were blocked, Surrealism could make its final contribution as the ideology of letting go of ideas. In his grasp of consciousness through immediate experience, the Surrealist painter stood directly opposed to the asceticism of Gorky as the pro-

Madame Donati, Marcel Duchamp, Maria Martins, Gorky, Frederick Kiesler. c. 1946.

vincial impersonator of The Great Artist. Looking everywhere, in the streets, in private relations, at parties, for their games of "black humor" and "chance meetings," they showed him that art and the artist were one. In view of his past, it would not be too much to say that in the company of the Surrealists Gorky was forced into life in order to be an artist. The secret, he learned, lay not in the rigors of emulation but in the gifts of insight, of which one's art was the unique record.

For art to serve revelation, picture-making as an ideal had to be dissolved. Instead of looking to art for direction, Gorky now turns to nature and to his own imagination: NON-ART FOR ART'S SAKE. For the first time he relaxes his striving for the master-work in favor of drawing and painting as a continuous note-taking of vision. No longer is the canvas conceived as an ideal entity standing above the artist as the alter ego of his "miserable" self; it is a record of the art activity to which its creator has surrendered.

Gorky now starts a drawing and looks to it for surprises. He experiments with close renderings of grass and flowers carried into fantasy by the spontaneous intervention of his hyper-trained hand. The loosening of the "classical" stranglehold has its strongest effect upon his composition. His formerly unyielding forms open to welcome the unexpected, the outrageous even. Tightly impacted organizations of carefully limited elements give way to litter and tiny afterthoughts. Details

seem thrown around, or thrown in for their own
sake, and one is aware of scattering and "disar-
ticulation." His paint no longer applies itself layer

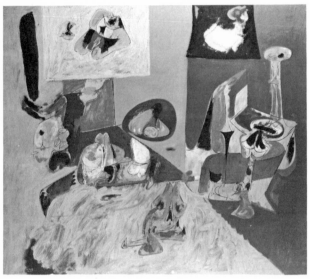

The Calendars. 1946-47. Oil. 50x60.
Destroyed by fire, Executive Mansion, Albany, 1961.

upon layer within an outlined area—it moves,
dabbles, spills, sometimes bursts up in a gust like
the flame of a match.

Literally beside himself, that is, acting outside
the limits of his self-consciousness, Gorky can now
make manifest in his painting and drawings psychological states he had formerly confided only in
private relations. Erotic signs flood his soul of a
Puritan. The sheltered space of *The Diary of a*

Seducer, The Betrothal, Charred Beloved, echoes back that cry of his love letters which is also an esthetic apperception: "this place seems so big without you." This typical sentiment of the stranger is unwound by his art into the vocabulary of world painting. Clinging to the local color of traditional painting, he encompasses an abstract figure ("you?" "me?") in a cavelike environment that could be either an interior or a landscape. A "place" of his own is born out of a combination of the seen and the half-thought. His sites seem *phrased* as much as composed, an assemblage of shapes that are also worlds. "Gorky's gardens flutter with a light and witty *loquacity*," wrote Elaine de Kooning, exactly divining his late landscapes to be a species of visual talk; where "in an overpowering flux of successive and simultaneous images, forms change, as you look, into a cruel and opulent sexual imagery. Accents of bright color suddenly lose their meaning as flowers, and become crevices, imparting a strange, voluptuous meaning to the surrounding pale, thinly washed surfaces; or plant forms change into human organs and a riotous pageant is transformed into a desolate landscape strewn with viscera. The general erotic content of his later work is suggested in some of his titles."

In Gorky's jottings of observed, fanciful, and spontaneously suggested shapes, pencil and crayon took on new importance. Recapturing without nostalgia the natural world he had lost since

Gorky with Marc Gorky and André Breton. c. 1946.

childhood, Gorky spent his summers drawing in the fields, the increasing fluidity of his penmanship garnering from the close scrutiny of weeds and the insides of flowers forms which, in being used again and again, became overgrown with metaphor and association. Amid strange, soft organisms and insidious slits and smudges, petals hint of claws in a jungle of limp bodily parts, intestinal fists, pubic discs, pudenda, multiple limbfolds, while angular braces evoke ribcases and African shields. Some of these drawings approach a resemblance to plates in botany books or Victorian fruit-and-flower clusters, though without losing their strangeness. Often Masson is looking over Gorky's shoulder. But he looks with amazement; for Masson's metamorphoses follow rational analogy, whereas Gorky's finds have taken him over the edge into the arbitrariness of the imagined.

His derivations from other painters do not cease; one might say that influences flow into him more freely than before. The difference is that they descend to the drawing board by way of the hand rather than the head. Whatever was original in the earlier Gorky was a remainder of his act of lodging himself in a pre-existing image— his originality in the forties is not of this order. For the first time, the totality of the work belongs to him, even when it is made up of borrowed parts. His eye freed from domination by the chosen model, he pours out its immediate data

Drawing for The Betrothal. 1946. Crayon. 19x24¾.
Courtesy Sidney Janis Gallery, New York.

upon his paper and canvas under the prompting
of visual and somatic memories of paintings which
he has seen or made. Art speaks anew through
these gestures, not as a concept but as an inspiring
Muse. The act of creation protracts itself with

undiminished spontaneity through innumerable references.

Gorky's vision now had its source within himself. Yet another still had to have a share in it, this time a share beyond the transactions of art. Gorky entered his new phase by way of the Chilean Surrealist Matta, this time responding not to a modern "old master" but to a painter younger and less skillful than himself. The effect of this new relationship upon Gorky proved far wider than that conveyed by the much-diluted word "influence." Matta not only succeeded Picasso and Miró as a guide to painting: he took the place of de Kooning and Reznikoff in another of Gorky's Mutt and Jeff pairs. Like his predecessors Matta resembled Gorky in being a foreigner and an artist; the identification was moved up a notch in his being also a non-European. Above all, Matta was fresh from Paris and wore the aura of Surrealism as the last movement in art, that is, as the most advanced point from which to go forward. In the most fateful sense, Matta became Gorky's "other." For a long time Gorky kept him to himself, evading the new arrival's efforts to meet other New York artists through him—I have been told that Matta even tried following him to his favorite restaurant in the hope of running into his friends there. But if Gorky was eager to preserve the new couple from intrusion, the short, rubicund Latin American—with his bright black eyes and his darting mind that revered cruel thoughts in the

Study for The Betrothal. 1946. Crayon. 49x39.
Collection Miss Jeanne Reynal.

Surrealist canon of the Marquis de Sade, the Rimbaud of *Une Saison,* and the imagery of Duchamp
and American comic strips—played his Jeff to the
hilt. Committed to moral provocations and ruses
of destruction, he made of his tall, melancholy

partner's sortie into life an induction into dis-
aster. As if personifying the dual forces of rejuve-
nation and death at work in Gorky, Matta pointed
the way for him to bring his art into touch with
his being, then did not hesitate to break his ego to
pieces by wilfully emerging into the desolation of
Gorky's illness as the focus of his violent jealousy.

Without this accomplice of his self-discovery
and his fate, the art of Gorky's last seven years
would not be what it is. Yet the Matta in Gorky's
painting belongs entirely to Gorky; here, at last,
was invention which he could consume and digest, as Picasso had cannibalized so many of his
contemporaries. The recurrence in his drawing of
Matta's curious elbow-joint shapes and cartoon flat-
tenings never transports his pictures into Matta's
world, as his borrowings from Cézanne and Miró
did into theirs. Matta's image is the rigid one of
ideological projection. In his paintings of that
period, line works as string in conjunction with
stretched planes to send flying machines or kites
adrift in angry-toned apocalypses of cloud dunes
and photographic smears. Later, he moved indoors
into a universal hospital ward of monochromatic
metal bugmen. Matta's ambition to be the me-
chanic of cosmic space and of man-as-equipment
did not tempt Gorky; the latter's canvases are not
wired for shock, nor are his compositions animated
by gas and pulleys. Having rid himself of the
ideology of art's-next-move, Gorky had become
content to comb the beaches where passion and

esthetic memories meet. With him "dismembered" composition is held to an order of planes inherited from his years of Cubist practice. His

The Betrothal II. 1947. Oil. 50¾x38.
Collection Whitney Museum of American Art.

landscapes are truly "interior," in that they resist external location, to say nothing of a "message." In the end, the argumentative Gorky turns out to be the most reticent of painters.

To Americans whose conception of abstract art was limited to the Cubist primer, the free intrusion of psychological subject matter was equivalent to mental collapse, if not a surrender to criminal tendencies. Stuart Davis, Gorky's defender in the early thirties, referring to the "moths sifted into his [Gorky's] prayer-type rug" by the Surrealists, concluded that he had "settled for a self on a lower level than the potential of his early noble pretensions. He retained his unusual mimetic and virtuoso-type technical talents but put them to the service of an inner landscape where gusts of some very loose-life literature obscured the vista." In a similar vein, another critic, later to emerge through timely adjustment as an early champion, if not "discoverer," of Gorky, had observed: "Gorky has at last taken the easy way out—corrupted perhaps by the example of the worldly success of the imported Surrealists and such Neo-Romantics as Tchelitchew . . . it all goes hand in hand with the renunciation of ambition." That Gorky was consciously establishing a new purpose for abstraction in the visual power of contours, strokes and color washes could not be grasped by those to whom abstract art meant geometrical patternings, overall design, "flat space."

Still often missed is the fact that the Surrealist

notations in Gorky's late paintings are but one element in them, often a superficial one. In perhaps half the painting from 1943 through 1948,

Soft Night. 1947. Oil. 37⅞x50.
Collection John Stephan.

figuration plays a negligible part: in several it is dispensed with altogether—the formal ground of his art is especially evident in sketches made for paintings, as distinguished from his nature studies and doodlings. At all times Gorky belongs to America's new abstract art, pre-figured by Kandinsky, rather than to a latter-day Surrealism. The relation to Kandinsky is very clear in paintings of '43-'44 such as *The Waterfall* and *The Liver is the Cock's Comb*, with the flowing edges of its forms; and it was in connection with the Connecticut scene that inspired some of these works that Gorky wrote of the "action of a rock," a perception quite acceptable to the esthetic imagination, though scientific estheticians are obliged to make distinctions between shapes of static objects and "dynamic" forms like waterfalls.

Dogmas and tendencies aside, however, *The Diary of a Seducer,* a composition of mixed "abstract" and figurative elements, and a product of the middle "last years," is to my mind Gorky's masterpiece. It combines most perfectly three qualities of some dozen paintings that are the culmination of Gorky's art: esthetic allusion, technical virtuosity, emotional content. This elegant grisaille echoes in the most contemporary terms the harmonies of the museum; rich in metaphors and visual puns it asserts the continuity of art without sacrifice of individal sensibility and without any trace of platitude or forcing, as legitimate a child of tradition and immediacy as a landscape of Cézanne. Ethel Schwabacher has related *The Diary* to Ingres' *Odalisque* in the Metropolitan; Elaine de Kooning found its composition pat with Ingres' source, J. L. David's *Mars Disarmed by Venus,* which Gorky had seen reproduced on the cover of a magazine. To me Gorky confided that the painting was of a landscape in Virginia. Probably all three statements are correct, since, given Gorky's method, his elaboration of the composition from sketches done on the site would have drawn in features of remembered masterpieces.

Related to other works of art and to nature, *The Diary* exhibits Gorky's manual freedom at its height. Its linear fluency addresses the masters it recalls with the modesty of an equal, while the

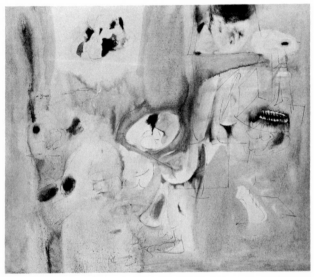

Making the Calendar. 1947. Oil. 34x41.
Collection Edward Root.

grand concavity of the whole, built of planes of gray peaked with points of bright color, is toned to a sense of endurance and to the subtleties of meditation.

As its title, contributed, we are told, by Max Ernst, suggests, this canvas is also a reflective autobiography (note, for instance, the boat or cradle-like shape carried over in miniature from *Garden in Sochi*). For is not the artist a "seducer," and has not the lone immigrant won his distinction solely through charm? In this "place" that is not "too big," internal organs palpitate and the mood is one of quiet expectation and anxiety.

In Kierkegaard's term, both the art of the past and the American landscape have become in *The Diary* "infinitely subjective." Signifying simultaneously on its multiple levels of the esthetic, of nature and of self-disclosure, *The Diary of a Seducer* is an equivalent in painting of a passage in *Finnegan's Wake* or one of the *Quartets* of Eliot.

Similar mastery is evident in such other Gorkys as *The Limit, Soft Night, Agony* (reproductions of this work, which falsify the reds, are particularly misleading). Several of the late works, however, do not succeed to the same degree in setting his figuration into the context of his entire vocabulary. Taken by themselves, his free associations can be mere rhetorical blubbering. Thus attempts to "read" Gorky's pictures for disclosures concerning the pathos of the flesh or the destiny of man seem ill-advised. Not in his metaphors but in the action of his hand in fastening them within their painting-concept lies the meaning of his work.

At the same time, Gorky differs from the Action Painters in that for him the gesture is never a sufficient starting point. His automatism is geared to creatures and scenes rather than to thrust, counter-movement and explosions of paint. This is so even when he gives himself most deeply to "expressive" abstraction, as in his "drip" paintings,

Composition. c. 1947. Oil. 11⅜x13.
Collection The New Gallery, Inc.

like the magnificent *Water of the Flowery Mill.* To the end, it is the clarified vision of the contemplator that manifests itself on his canvas, not the tangled or locked masses experienced by the participant. He observes the image that rises before him: he does not "get into it" as into an arena. Psychologically, Gorky's paintings constitute an investigation of the unknown, rather than an immersion in its currents; their aim is the conversion of data through esthetic comprehension, rather than an organization of the artist's energy as in de Kooning, Kline, Hofmann, Guston.

Yet Gorky was a pioneer in discovering the primary principles of America's new abstract art. For him abstract art meant, finally, not abstracting from experience but making experience over through a protracted series of connected efforts; a sketch was an event which led to another, not a draft to be perfected. For him, as for the Action Painters, the canvas was not a surface upon which to present an image, but a "mind" through which the artist discovers, by means of manual and mental hypotheses, signs of what he is or might be. To this "mind" Gorky brought accumulations of the hand that reveal him to be in fact the artist he had begun by inventing.

NOTES

1. Ethel K. Schwabacher, *Arshile Gorky* (Whitney Museum, 1957).
2. Stuart Davis, "Arshile Gorky in the 1930's: A Personal Recollection," *Magazine of Art*, February, 1951.
3. "Fetish of Antique Stifles Art Here, Says Gorky Kin," *New York Evening Post*, February 15, 1926.
4. Letter of Willem de Kooning to *Art News*, January, 1949.
5. Elaine de Kooning, "Gorky: Painter of his own Legend," *Art News*, January, 1951.
6. WPA Statement by Gorky, (see Appendix).
7. See "The American Action Painters," *Tradition of the New*, by Harold Rosenberg (Horizon Press, 1959).

CHRONOLOGY OF GORKY'S LIFE

1905   Arshile Gorky (baptized Vosdanig Adoian) born at Hayotz Dzore in Turkish Armenia; father, a wheat trader and carpenter.

1920   Arrives in United States with a party of Armenian immigrants. Lives in Providence and Boston until 1925.

1920-25   Series of still-lifes and portraits influenced by Cézanne. Studies at Rhode Island School of Design, Providence Technical High School, and New School of Design in Boston.

1925   Vosdanig Adoian changes his name to Arshile Gorky. Moves to New York City, taking a studio on Sullivan Street near Washington Square. Studies at Grand Central School of Art, teaches there until 1931.

1926   Begins *The Artist and His Mother* under the influence of Ingres. Pre-Cubist period: *Antique Cast*, influenced by Braque and Picasso.

1927-32	Experiments with Cubist still-lifes, declaring: "Has there in six centuries been better art than Cubism? No. Centuries will go past —artists of gigantic stature will draw positive elements from Cubism" (1931).
1929	Friendship with Stuart Davis.
1930	First museum showing in Museum of Modern Art exhibition, "46 Painters and Sculptors under 35." Moves to new studio at 36 Union Square, New York.
1932	Becomes member of the "Abstraction, Creation, Art Non-Figuratif" group in Paris, including Albers, Calder, Hélion, etc.
1933-36	*Organization* series. Begins long friendship with Willem de Kooning.
1934	First one-man show (February) at Mellon Galleries, Philadelphia. Termination of his association with Stuart Davis.
1935	Joins WPA Federal Art Project: begins *Aviation* murals for Newark Airport. First marriage, to Marny George, divorced soon after.
1936	First magazine article on Gorky, by Frederick Kiesler, in *Art Front*, Dec. 18, 1936. Four versions of *Image of Xhorkom*.
1937	First museum purchase: Whitney Museum, *Painting*, 1936-37.
1938	First one-man show of paintings in New York, at Boyer Galleries.
1938-42	Eight versions of *Garden in Sochi*.
1939	*Aviation* murals for New York World's Fair.
1941	Second marriage, to Agnes Magruder (Sept. 15), in Virginia City, Nevada. Retrospective exhibition of twenty paintings at San Francisco Museum of Art.
1942	First visit to Connecticut, at Saul Schary's home.

1943	*Waterfall.* Frequent visits to parents-in-law's farm in Hamilton, Virginia, through 1946.
1944	*The Liver Is the Cock's Comb.* Meets André Breton and Surrealist emigrés in New York.
1945	*Diary of a Seducer.* Exhibits at Julien Levy Gallery, New York (January), and shows annually there through 1948.
1946	About twenty-seven of his paintings destroyed by fire (January) in his studio at Sherman, Conn. Operated on for cancer (February).
1946-47	*The Calendars.*
1947	Settles permanently in Sherman, Conn. (December). *The Plow and the Song, Agony, Betrothal I* and *II, The Orators, Soft Night.*
1948	*Last Painting.* Neck broken and painting arm paralyzed in automobile accident (June 26). Commits suicide, by hanging, at his farm in Sherman (July 21).

FETISH OF ANTIQUE

STIFLES ART HERE

Arshele Gorky, twenty-three-year-old Russian painter, has been claimed by New York for her own, and today he became an active member of the faculty of the Grand Central School of Art.

The election of Mr. Gorky to the art school faculty gives New York indefinitely, perhaps permanently, a member of one of Russia's greatest artist families, for he is a cousin of the famous writer, Maxim Gorky. But Arshele Gorky's heart and soul are still his own.

He gives New York his facile, talented hand and laughs at its blustering pretensions that it is an overpowering city bound to make a deep impression upon a young foreign artist.

After two years of studying and painting in the gigantic rush of the most staggering city in the world, Arshele Gorky, in his studio in the shadow of towering skyscrapers, is working today on a still life study of a few glass objects and some fruit. And it isn't only skyscrapers—Mr. Gorky hit at another American institution, too.

"The greatest barrier to recognition of important young artists in America is the American craze for antiques," he told a reporter for this paper.

But that criticism is only one of a number of thoughtful comments that the young Russian has to make of art as it is practiced in America and as it is regarded by Americans.

"America must always have antique things, always old masters, always big names," he said. "Your museums are filled with antiques, your art dealers emphasize antiques, and do not become protagonists of the greater modern art because of helping the antique craze along."

The stigma of "well known" is another handicap to modern art in America, he pointed out. The young artist, crowded out by antique dealers and big names, has little opportunity to exhibit his work in New York and other cities, according to Mr. Gorky.

"In Paris and in Germany," he said, "a painting done this year is exhibited this year. There are museums and exhibitions given over to the progress of the living, modern, growing art, but in America you ask 'How old is it?' or 'Do I know the name signed to it?' before it has a chance."

Ranged about the Gorky Studio in West Fiftieth street are many quiet still life paintings; many portraits of persons who are not "well-known," many landscapes. But you will look in vain for the devastating influence of the Woolworth building, or for Broadway and Forty-second street on Saturday night.

"Art is not in New York you see; art is in you. Atmosphere is not something New York has, it is also in you," the artist says.

With a wave of his long, thin hand he disposed of the greatest city in the world. For all the effect it has had upon his art he might have spent the last two years in Winesburg, O., or some village in France or darkest Russia even.

He spoke of the effect of commercial lures upon the young American artist subjected to the attraction of money.

"But a real artist, of course, cares not what he sells any more than where he is. If a painting of mine suits me, it is right. If it does not please me, I care not if all the great masters should approve it or the dealers buy it. They would be wrong. How could there be anything fine in my painting unless I put it there and see it?"

Americans follow the "smart," Mr. Gorky says, and, that, too, he believes militates against a fair and impartial judgment of the modern art he calls the greatest the world has known.

"Your Twachtman painted a waterfall that was a waterfall in any country, as Whistler's mother was any one's mother. He caught the universal idea of art. Art is always universal. It is not New England or the South or New York."

Again his gesture scorned the roar outside his windows.

"Too many American artists paint portraits that are portraits of a New Yorker, but not of the human being."

Dismissal of modern painting, of the work of Cezanne and Matisse and Picasso as "crazy," is, in Arshele Gorky's opinion, the worst of all possible mistakes.

"These men are greater artists than the old masters," he said. "Cezanne is the greatest artist, shall I say, that has lived. The old masters were bound by convention and rule to painting certain things—saints, the Madonna, the crucifixion. Modern art has gone ahead widely and developed as it never had a chance to in the hands of the old masters. And there are many good artists in America—there are many fine appreciators of art, men who are doing much for art."

The young Russian hears occasionally from his famous cousin, Maxim, who is now in Venice, treating a cardiac ailment and writing.

The art school in which M. Gorky teaches is on the seventh floor of the Grand Central terminal building. You take an elevator at track 29 and are whirled above the thundering labyrinth of one of America's vastest speed industries. It is doubtful if the young Russian painter knows it is there.

It is after all a very small thing. Like, say, a siding in a little Russian town.

—*New York Evening Post, Sept. 15, 1926.*

STUART DAVIS

By Arshele Gorky

. . . Yet the silent consequences of Stuart Davis move us to the cool and intellectual world where all human emotions are disciplined upon rectangular proportions. Here these relations take us to the scientific world where all dreams evaporate and logic plays its greatest victory, where the physical world triumphs over all tortures, where all the clumsiness dies, and leaves only the elements of virtue, where the esthetic world takes new impulse for new consequences. Oh, what a glorious prospect! This man, this American, this pioneer, this modest painter, who never disarranges his age, who works to perfect his motives, who renders—clear, more definite, more and more decided—new forms and new objects. He chooses new rules to discipline his emotions. He gives new shape to his experiences with new sequences—orange, red, yellow, green, brown and chalk-like white, metallic grays and dull blacks, profound spaces with sky-like blues, stabilized upon rectangular directions. He takes a new position upon the visible world. This artist, whether he paints egg-beaters, streets, or pure geometrical organizations, expresses his constructive attitude toward his successive experiences. He gives us symbols of tangible spaces, with gravity and physical law. He, above his contemporaries, rises high—mountain-like! Oh, what clarity! One he is, and one of but few, who realizes his canvas as a rectangular shape with two dimensional surface plane. Therefore he forbids himself to poke bumps and holes upon that potential surface. This man, Stuart Davis, works upon that platform where are working the giant painters of the century—Picasso, Leger, Kandinsky, Juan Gris—bringing to us new utility, new aspects, as does the art of Uccello. They take us to the supernatural world behind reality where once the great centuries danced.

Yet there are large numbers of critics, artists, and public suspended like vultures, waiting in the air for the death of the distinctive art of this century, the art of Leger, Picasso, Miro, Kandinsky, Stuart Davis. They forget that while the artist never works outside his time, yet his art will go on to be merged gradually into the new art of a new age. There will be no short stop. We shall not, contrary to the expectation of these people, hear of the sudden death of Cubism, abstraction, so-called modern art. These critics, these artists, these spectators who wait for a sudden fall are doomed to disappointment. They have merely not understood the spiritual movement and the law of direct energy of the centuries, and they can never have understood the spiritual meaning of any form of art. If they could but realize that energy is a spiritual movement and that they must conceive of working under a law of universal esthetic progress, as we do in science, in mathematics, in physics.

The twentieth century—what intensity, what activity,

what restless nervous energy! Has there in six centuries been better art than Cubism? No. Centuries will go past—artists of gigantic stature will draw positive elements from Cubism.

Clumsy painters take a measurable space, a clear definite shape, a rectangle, a vertical or horizontal direction, and they call it blank canvas, while every time one stretches canvas he is drawing a new space. How could they ever have understood Cubism or the art of the twentieth century? How could they even conceive of the elements that go into the making of art? How could they accept tranquility and expansion as elements of feeling in painting?

—*Originally published in* Creative Art, *vol. 9 (Sept. 1931), pp. 213-17.*

THE WPA MURALS
AT THE NEWARK AIRPORT

The architectonic two-dimensional surface plane of walls must be retained in mural painting. How was I to overcome this plastic problem when the subject of my murals was that of the unbounded space of the sky-world of aviation? How keep the walls from flying away or else crushing together as they would be sure to do in a pictorial narrative? The problem resolved itself when I considered the new vision that flight has given to the eyes of man. The isle of Manhattan with all its skyscrapers from the view of an aeroplane five miles up becomes but a geographical map, a two-dimensional surface plane. This new perception simplifies the form and shapes of earth objects. The thickness of objects is lost and only the space occupied by the objects remains. Such simplification removes all decorative details and leaves the artist with limitations which become a style, a plastic invention, particular to our time. How was I to utilize this new concept for my murals?

In the popular idea of art, an aeroplane is painted as it might look in a photograph. But such a hackneyed concept has no architectural unity in the space that it is to occupy nor does it truthfully represent an aeroplane with all its ramifications. An operation was imperative, and that is why in the first panel of "Activities on the Field" I had to dissect an aeroplane into its constituent parts. An aeroplane is composed of a variety of shapes and forms and I have used such elemental forms as a rudder, a wing, a wheel, a searchlight, etc., to create not only numerical interest, but also to include within a given wall space, plastic symbols of aviation. These plastic symbols are the permanent elements of aeroplanes that will change with the change of design. These symbols, these forms, I have used in paralyzing disproportions in order to impress upon the spectator the miraculous new vision of our time. To add to the intensity of these shapes, I have used such local colors as are to be seen on the aviation field, red, blue, yellow, black, gray, brown, because these colors were used originally to sharpen the objects against neutral backgrounds so that they could be seen clearly and quickly.

The second panel of the same wall contains objects commonly used around a hangar, such as a ladder, a fire extinguisher, a gasoline truck, scales, etc. These objects I have dissected and reorganized in the same homogeneous arrangement as in the previous panel.

In the panel "Early Aviation," I sought to bring into elemental terms the sensation of the passengers in the first balloon to the wonder of the sky around them and the earth beneath. Obviously this conception entails a different problem than those previously cited. In fact each of the walls presents a different problem concerning aviation and to solve each one, I had to use different concepts, different plastic qualities, different colors. Thus, to appreciate my panel of the first balloon, the spectator must seek to imaginatively enter into the miraculous sense of wonder experienced by the first balloonists. In the shock of surprise everything changes. The sky becomes green. The sun is black with astonishment on beholding an invention never before created by the hand of God. And the earth is spotted with such elliptical brown forms as had never been seen before.

This image of wonder I continued in the second panel. From the first balloon of Mongolfier, aviation developed until the wings of the modern aeroplane, figuratively speaking, stretch across the United States. The sky is still green for the wonders of the sky never cease, and the map of the United States takes on a new geographical outline because of the illusion of change brought about by the change in speed.

The first three panels of "Modern Aviation" contain the anatomical parts of autogyros in the process of soaring into space, and yet with the immobility of suspension. The fourth panel is a modern aeroplane simplified to its essential form and so spaced as to give a sense of flight.

In the last three panels I have used arbitrary colors and shapes; the wing is black, the rudder yellow, so as to convey the sense that these modern gigantic toys of men are decorated with the same fanciful play as children have in coloring their kites. In the same spirit the engine becomes in one place like the wings of a dragon and in another the wheels, propeller and motor take on the demonic speed of a meteor cleaving the atmosphere.

In "Mechanics of Flying" I have used morphic shapes. The objects portrayed, a thermometer, hygrometer, anemometer, an aeroplane map of the United States, all have a definitely important usage in aviation, and to emphasize this, I have given them importance by detaching them from their environment."

—"*Aviation: Evolution of Forms under Aerodynamic Limitations.*"

CAMOUFLAGE:

An epidemic of destruction sweeps the world today. The mind of civilized man is set to stop it. What the enemy would destroy, however, he must first see. To confuse and paralyze this vision is the role of camouflage. Here the artist and more particularly the modern artist can fulfill a vital function for opposed to this vision of destruction is the vision of creation.

Historically, it has been the artist's role to make manifest the beautiful inherent in all the objects of nature and man. In the study of the object, as a thing seen, he has acquired a profound understanding and sensibility concerning its visual aspects. The philosophy as well as the physical and psychological laws governing their relationships constitutes the primary source material for the study of camouflage. The mastery of this visual intelligence has been the particular domain of the modern artist. Intent on the greatest exploration of the visible world it was the Cubist painters who created the new magic of space and color that everywhere today confronts our eyes in new architecture and design. Since then the various branches of modern art through exhaustive experiment and research have created a vast laboratory whose discoveries unveiled for all the secrets of form, line and color. For it is these elements that make an object visible and which are for the artist the vocabulary of his language.

Arshile Gorky, himself a product of this period and a modern painter of considerable reputation, will add to this material his studies and knowledge in the field of science. Particularly pertinent, and forming the second source for the understanding of camouflage, is the data on protective coloring in zoology, optical illusion in the physics of light, and visual reactions to movement in Gestalt psychology. To complete the instruction and give it proper perspective is the history of camouflage and its application in the past.

The Grand Central School of Art is very glad of this opportunity to extend its facilities to Mr. Gorky for this extremely interesting course.

Using these facilities, Mr. Gorky plans a studio workshop in which every student becomes a discoverer. Original research will be carried out by students in new phases of camouflage through the observation of a theory and practice method of instruction. Work in new materials, the making of scale-models, and the building of abstract constructions will be related to group discussions and lectures. Forming the ideological background will be studies in the history and aesthetics of modern art. Because of the urgent pressure of current events, the course will be a living one. Invited authorities, as well as scientists will demonstrate and confer with workshop groups.

This course is dedicated to that artist, contemporary in his understanding of forces in the modern world, who would use this knowledge in a function of in-

creasing importance. Such an artist will gain a knowledge that will deepen and enrich his understanding
of art as well as make him an important contributor
to civilian and military defense.

Registration fee $5.00—Tuition $15.00 per month.
Day and evening classes.

ARSHILE GORKY: *Born in Russia: Studied art at Julian
Academy, also at various schools in Paris, Providence,
Boston, New York, etc. Studied engineering at Poly-
technic Institute, Tiflis, Russia. Pictures in important
collections and museums of France and United States.
Taught at Grand Central School of Art and privately.
Lectured at colleges and museums throughout the
country. Murals executed for Newark Airport and
Aviation Building at World's Fair.*

FAREWELL TO ARSHILE GORKY

By André Breton

How big you were with your arms opened
Your voice was an eagle's nest
When you sang to yourself the old Russian Songs
You had received as your share the pure line
More than you knew what to do with
And the heavy net which you were bringing back alone
From the depth of ages
In long armfuls mingled the season's charms and the
    memories
You should have been seen with the landscape
You and the splendid blindman who shadowed you
The figurative and the non-figurative
It's you who crumbled that dry bread
I see you again with your rod of fables
Among the stars and the flowering trees
I tear myself from your destiny
How they clung to you dear Arshile
Ah he loves fire where is his house burn it

It and what he keeps in it as evidence of twenty years
 of disinterested efforts torn away from all that is seen
 today you tempt me damn him said the ash to the
 ember
And as if this were not enough
They insisted on putting some of your own red on the
 spot of the sun of your body
Then as you were returning
They ambushed you to break your neck
At that most tender place where your fairy-child
 perched
So both together could see further
Who knows if they didn't have more tricks up their
 sleeve
You had nothing left
But to take for yourself the magical death of Gerard
 de Nerval
How high you are
In the air
Less than in what you leave us
Less than in your name
Aimed at the great storms of my heart

—Translated by Denise Hare

SELECTED BIBLIOGRAPHY

*(Place of publication is New York City,
unless otherwise indicated)*

BOOKS

Baur, John I. H. *Revolution and Tradition in Modern
   American Art.* Cambridge, Mass: 1951, pp. 70-71.
   1 ill.
Blesh, Rudi. *Modern Art USA.* 1956, pp. 132, 244-45,
   257-59. 3 ill.
Breton, André. *Le Surréalisme et la Peinture.* 1945, pp.
   196-97. 1 ill.
Collection of the Société Anonyme. New Haven: Yale
   University Art Gallery, 1950, pp. 34-35. 1 ill.
Goodrich, Lloyd. "Arshile Gorky," in *New Art in
   America,* ed. John I. H. Baur. Greenwich, Conn:
   1957, pp. 188-91. 4 ill.
Hess, Thomas B. *Abstract Painting.* 1951, pp. 5, 105-6,
   108-11. 4 ill.
Janis, Sidney. *Abstract & Surrealist Art in America.*
   1944, pp. 89, 120. 1 ill.

Rodman, Selden. *The Eye of Man.* 1955, pp. 122, 136, 137. 1 ill.

Schwabacher, Ethel K. *Arshile Gorky.* 1957. 76 ill.

REVIEWS AND ARTICLES

1936

"Arshile Gorky Exhibits," *Art Digest,* vol. 10, p. 21.

Kiesler, Frederick J. "Murals Without Walls," *Art Front,* vol. 2 (December), pp. 10-11. 2 ill. (The Newark Airport Project).

Lane, James W. "Current Exhibitions," *Parnassus,* vol. 8 (March), p. 27.

1938

"L'Art Contemporain aux Etats-Unis," *Cahiers d'Art* (Paris), vol. 13, nos. 1-2, p. 51. 1 ill.

1944

Sweeney, James Johnson. "Five American Painters," *Harper's Bazaar,* vol. 78 (April), pp. 122, 124. 1 ill.

1945

Coates, Robert. "The Art Galleries," *New Yorker,* vol. 21 (March 17), p. 77.

Greenberg, Clement. "Art," *Nation,* vol. 160 (March 24), pp. 342-43.

"The Passing Shows," *Art News,* vol. 44 (March 15), p. 24.

Riley, Maude. "The Eye-Spring: Arshile Gorky," *Art Digest,* vol. 19 (March 15), p. 10.

1946

Greenberg, Clement. "Art," *Nation,* vol. 162 (May 4), pp. 552-53.

Reed, Judith Kaye. "Salvaged from Fire," *Art Digest,* vol. 20 (May 1), p. 13.

"Reviews and Previews," *Art News,* vol. 45 (April), p. 54.

Sunley, Robert. "Fourteen American Artists," *Critique,* vol. 1 (October), p. 21.

1947

Lansford, Alonzo. "Concentrated Doodles," *Art Digest,* vol. 21 (March), p. 18.

"Reviews and Previews," *Art News,* vol. 46 (March), p. 43.

1948

Greenberg, Clement. "Art," *Nation,* vol. 166 (January 10), p. 52.

————"Art," *Nation,* vol. 166 (March 20), pp. 331-32.

————"Art Chronicle," *Partisan Review,* vol. 15 (March), p. 369. 2 ill.

————"Art," *Nation,* vol. 167 (December 11), p. 676.

"Reviews and Previews," *Art News,* vol. 47 (March), p. 46.

————*Art News,* vol. 47 (December), pp. 53-54.

1950

Barr, Alfred H. Jr. "7 Americans Open in Venice," *Art News,* vol. 49 (Summer), pp. 22, 60. 1 ill.

Breuning, Margaret. "A Memorial for Arshile Gorky," *Art Digest,* vol. 24 (April), p. 18. 1 ill.

Greenberg, Clement. "Art Chronicle," *Partisan Review,* vol. 17 (May-June), pp. 512-13.

Hess, Thomas B. "Reviews and Previews," *Art News,* vol. 49 (April), p. 45. 1 ill.

Kees, Weldon. "Art," *Nation,* vol. 170 (April 8), p. 334.

Louchheim, Aline. "Contemporary Art in New York," *Atlantic Monthly,* vol. 186 (December), pp. 65-66.

1951

"Arshile Gorky," *Art Digest,* vol. 25 (February 1), p. 19.

Ballard, Louise. "Art," *Art and Architecture* (Los Angeles), vol. 68 (May), pp. 10-11.

Coates, Robert. "The Art Galleries," *New Yorker,* vol. 26 (January 20), pp. 60, 62-63.

Curl, Huldah. "Arshile Gorky Memorial Exhibition, Walker Art Center, Minneapolis," *Notes and Comments,* vol. 5 (March), pp. 1-2. 1 ill.

de Kooning, Elaine. "Gorky: Painter of His Own Legend," *Art News,* vol. 49 (January), pp. 38-41, 63-66.

"Fiery River of Images," *Pictures on Exhibit,* vol. 13 (January), pp. 4-5. 2 ill.

Goodnough, Robert. "Arshile Gorky," *Art News,* vol. 49 (February), p. 46.

Goodrich, Lloyd. "Notes on 8 Works by Arshile Gorky," *Magazine of Art,* vol. 44 (February), p. 46.

"Gorky: Was He Tops or Second Rate?" *Art Digest,* vol. 25 (January 15), pp. 9, 30. 3 ill.

Soby, James Thrall. "Arshile Gorky," *Magazine of Art,* vol. 44 (February), p. 56.

"Whitney Honors Gorky," *Art Digest,* vol. 25 (January 1), p. 6.

1953

Coates, Robert. "The Art Galleries," *New Yorker,* vol. 27 (February), p. 83.

Fitzsimmons, James. "The Late Gorky," *Art Digest,* vol. 27 (March), p. 16.

McBride, Henry. "Success at Last," *Art News,* vol. 52 (April), pp. 66-67.

"Spirit, Time and 'Abstract Expressionism,'" *Magazine of Art,* vol. 46 (February), pp. 82-84. 3 ill.

1954

"Arshile Gorky's *The Plow and The Song*," *Allen Memorial Art Museum Bulletin*, vol. 12 (Fall), pp. 4-15. 5 ill.

Feinstein, Sam. "A Gallery Itinerary," *Art Digest*, vol. 28 (April 15), p. 21.

Porter, Fairfield. "Arshile Gorky," *Art News*, vol. 53 (April), p. 53.

Krasne, Belle. "Nine American Painters, Nine American Worlds," *Art Digest*, vol. 28 (January 15), pp. 10-12.

1955

Art News, vol. 54 (November), p. 50.

"Gorky, Matta, de Kooning, Pollock," *Arts Digest*, vol. 29 (June 1), p. 24.

Kramer, Hilton. "Month in Review," *Arts*, vol. 30 (October), pp. 48-49.

1957

Arti Visive (Rome), nos. 6-7. Bi-lingual issue devoted to Gorky.

1959

Jouffroy, Alain. "Arshile Gorky et les secrets de la nuit," *Cahiers du Musee De Poche* (Paris), No. 2 (June).

REMINISCENCES

Balamuth, Lewis. "I Met A. Gorky," *Color and Rhyme*, vol. 19 (1949).

Breton, André. "L'Adieu à Arshile Gorki" (Poem), Catalogue of Galerie Rene Drouin (Paris), undated.

Burliuk, Mary. "Arshile Gorky," *Color and Rhyme*, vol. 19 (1949).

Cowley, Malcolm. "Arshile Gorky—A Note from A Friend," New York *Herald Tribune*, September 5, 1948, sec. 6, p. 3.

Davis, Stuart. "Arshile Gorky in the 1930's: A Personal Recollection," *Magazine of Art*, vol. 44 (February, 1951).

————"Handmaiden of Misery," *The Saturday Review*, vol. 40, no. 52 (December 28, 1957).

Denby, Edwin. "Recollections," in *The 30's*. Poindexter Gallery, 1957.

Ferren, John. "A Meeting with Gorky in 1938," in *The 30's*.

Mooradian, Karlen. "Arshile Gorky," *Armenian Review* (Boston), vol. 8 (Summer, 1955).

Phillips, Agnes ("Mougouch"). Letter from Gorky's widow, dated December 29, 1956, in *The 30's*.

ACKNOWLEDGMENTS

The author wishes especially to thank Rosalind Irvine of the Whitney Museum of American Art for her help in making material available; also Bernard Karpel, Librarian of The Museum of Modern Art. The chronology was prepared by William Berkson in connection with some excerpts from this book which appeared in *Portfolio*.